RAMBLINGS OF MY HEART

A Book of Poems and Thoughts
By Nancy Ann

This is a collection of poems, thoughts, short stories, and art. I hope you enjoy them.

Many of my poems might be dark and depressing, but writing is how I cope with things life throws at us. When I'm frustrated, hurt, and sad, I write. It helps me cope with my feelings though not every poem will fit this description most of them will.

I write on a slew of subjects; motherhood, family, miscarriage, children, raising children and many more. Sometimes moms get into a competition of who's the better mother or who has the best kids, whose job is hard, and that mindset helps no one. So, I promise to be as real as I can, hoping the things that have challenged me can help someone else.

© 2022 by Nancy Ann all rights reserved. No section of *Ramblings of my heart* shall be duplicated, translated in any form or by any means, or kept in any retrieval systems. Unauthorized use and/or duplication of this material without expressed and written permission from the author and owner is strictly prohibited. Excerpts may be used, provided that full and clear credit is given to Nancy Ann and *Ramblings of My Heart* with appropriate and specific direction to the original content.

Published by Amazon
ISBN
Printed in the
United States of
America

Other Books by Nancy Ann

When is it Enough?

The Fear

Life is too Short

Looking Back

Be Courageous Enough to Walk Away

When You…

I Don't Give a Fuck

I am Tired

Too Young

Pray

The Lake

Maybe

Out of the Grasp of a Loss

I Lost a Friend Today

The Only Job That Matters

What Can Be Done?

It is Okay to Cry!

My Soul Sings

Wake the Dragon

Honesty and Fear

I am Frustrated with Myself

The World is a Dark and Gloomy Place for Them.

Secrets

Why Do People Give Up on Me?

When is Enough, Enough?

My Baby

Sometimes

Only A Number

Meaningless

Things Done for Good

All a Lie

They Say

I am Strong

What Depression Feels Like

I See the Phone

Give Up

My Surprise

His Surprise

A Flower

Always

About the Author

Other Books by Nancy Ann

1. Birth After Miscarriage
2. The Shadow Realm Chronicles: Maeve
3. The Shadow Realm Chronicles: Matthew
4. The Shadow Realm Chronicles: Justin
5. The Shadow Realm Chronicles: Maurelle
6. Ramblings of the Mind
7. Ramblings of the Soul
8. Ramblings of the Spirit
9. Ramblings of the Heart
10. Rambling of a Chaotic Mind
11. The Adventures of Zelda and Foxy Roxy
12. The Adventures of Van and Bunny
13. The Adventures of Orion and Puppy
14. The Adventures of Zelda and Foxy Roxy: A Story about Autism
15. The Adventures of Van and Bunny: A Tale of Two Kitties
16. The Adventures of Orion and Puppy: The Story of Penny and Harper
17. The Adventures of Zelda and Foxy: Taking Care of Your Cat
18. The Creed of the Chrononauts: A Chrononauts Novel
19. Flight 532

Coming Soon

1. The Adventures of Van and Bunny: Van goes to the Hospital
2. The Shadow Realm Chronicles: Annabelle
3. The Shadow Realm Chronicles: Marius
4. The Creed of the Chronaunts: Into the West

When is it Enough?

How long do you reach out to someone?
How long do you call someone a friend?
Do you continue to pray even when they don't care about you?

When they tarnish your name,
When they won't talk to you,
When they ignore you,
How long do you wait?

Do you still pray?
Is it wrong to move on and not care?
Isn't it hard not to care?

Are you a horrible person if you move on?
Why do I feel guilty?
Shouldn't you pray for your enemies and friends alike?
Shouldn't you be the better person?

When is it enough?
When will it ever be enough?

The Fear

The fear of this reality.
The fear of life and its end.
The fear it builds in us, and we don't even realize it.
The fear we have, so we don't live our lives.

The fear we have that sits with us every day.
The fear that keeps us in doors.
The fear that keeps me from the hug.

The fear that we are not in control.
The fear no matter what we do, grabs us and binds us to it.
The fear that all I do may not be enough.
The realization that it will never be enough.

I lift my fears to you, my Lord.

I lift them to you, please take them.
For I am not in control.

Life is too Short

Don't hold grudges. Don't waste time.
Life is too short and unpredictable.
Don't hold grudges. Don't waste time.

Life is too short, to hold on to childish things.
Love like it is your last day.
Love and you will never be wrong.
Don't worry about trivial things.

Don't worry about who should say sorry.
Don't worry, just love.

Looking Back

Looking back, I wonder where I went wrong.
Looking back, I can see it was a facade.

It is difficult to see that it was fake.
It is difficult to see that I was the fool.
It is difficult to realize all of these things,
And still miss the past.

Looking back now it is clearer.
Looking back now I can see,
But it still hurts.

I wonder how to go on trusting.
I wonder how to go on building new relationships.
I wonder how to learn to trust again.

Be Courageous Enough to Walk Away

Sometimes it's better to walk away.
Walk away with your head held high.

It takes more courage to move on than to fight.
It takes more courage to admit defeat, but
is walking away really a defeat.

Is it defeat to move on?
Is it a defeat to move away from toxicity?
Is it defeat to want better? To want more?

Put your strength in things that matter,

not things that tear you down.

Sometimes it is better to walk away.

When You...

When you put yourself out there...
When you stand up for someone...
When you say what everyone else is thinking...
When I defend you...

Why is it that when I do these things, it always backfires?
Why is it that when I defend someone, I am the one in the wrong?
Why is it when I have your back, you don't have mine?
Why do I even bother?

I Don't Give a Fuck

We worry so much about what others think.
We watch things happen and never speak.
We never speak our mind.

When we do speak, people become upset.
As if we have no right to speak our mind.
We have no right to stand up for someone,
As if our views do not matter.

I'm tired of keeping quiet and worrying.
What if I say the wrong thing?
What if someone gets mad at me?

I have always been worried about
what people think of me.
Would people hate me? Would
they stop being my friend?

Today I say, I don't give a fuck.
If you don't like what I say, stop
talking to me.
If what I say, offends you so badly
that you need to end a friendship,
Then you were never my friend.

I don't give a fuck.
I will speak my mind.

I am Tired

I am tired of pretending that I am okay when I'm not.
I am tired of trying to be someone that I'm not.
You don't like me as I am; you want me to change, but why.
I am tired of making excuses for how I act.
Why did I try to work on things when no one else cares?

I am tired of being lonely but if that is what I have to do to be myself so be it.
I am angry and want to last out but it won't matter.

Nothing I say or do matters to them.
They don't care what happens to me.

I want to cry and lay on the bed all day, but it won't solve anything.
I want to lash out, but it won't matter.
Nothing matters.

Too Young

Failure, disappointment and regret.
There is an ache in my heart each time we lose another.
For all that are lost, this despair won't dissolve.

How could we have done more?
What could I have done?
Why do so many lives end this way?

The pain and sickening feeling each time I get the news.
Another one lost, and still another.
What can be done, when so many are lost.

What can we do to stop this?
Too young to be a statistic.

30

Pray

When you know someone is not acting like they should.
When you know they are taking things out on others.
When you are their target, you should pray.

Pray for your soul as well as theirs.
Pray unceasing for their soul as well.
Pray for their clarity.

Pray so you no longer hold hatred in your heart.
Pray that you can have peace in your soul.
Pray for forgiveness and compassion.

You know something is wrong; you know they are not themselves.
You know they are not acting as they should.
You need to pray.

You need to pray even if people don't like you.
You need to pray, even if they don't want you to.
You need to pray and never stop.

The Lake

The cool water laps on my feet.
The sun rays warm my skin,
The birds chirp, the waters laps
And my soul is at ease.

So much noise in our lives.
So little time to unwind,
To be quiet in his presence
And soak in the son.

I bury my feet in the sand and,
I stretch my legs out.
The birds chirp, the waters laps
And my soul is at ease.

So much drama in our lives.
So little time to cry.
To be sheltered by his love
And know you are not alone.

Maybe

My heart aches,
You say everyone has an issue with me.
My fear all along and now I know.

Maybe I am not meant to have friends.
Maybe I am better off on my own.
Maybe you're lying. But maybe you're not.

Maybe they all hate me.
Maybe I am everything you say
Maybe everyone will be better if I disappear.

36

Out of the Grasp of a Loss

Out of the grasp of a loss
There is hope.
Out of the pain of loss.
There is hope.
Out of a broke trust
There is hope.

To start a new,
And live each day
With hope.

Build new friendships,
And forget about the ones you lost.
Nourish old friendships,
so, they become anew.
Build people up,
and show them you care.

You will never be alone,
But I know that is what you fear.

You fear being left alone, cast aside as
you have been before.
You fear not being good enough and
losing once more.

Build new friendships,
And forget about the ones you lost.
Nourish old friendships,
So, they become anew.
Build people up,
and show them you care.
And you will never be alone.

I Lost a Friend Today

I lost a friend today.
I should feel sad,
But I don't.

I lost a friend today.
I should be sad,
But I am glad.

Words were exchanged,
And I held my own.
Words were exchanged,
And I held my own.

No matter who you are,
There is a time and a place.
Friends should support others.
Those closest to you, should support you.
When they don't it is time to remove them from your life.

Everyone in your boat may not be
rowing for you, but against you.
As your success grows, their
loyalty fades.
They would rather push you down,
then see you succeed.

So today I lost a friend,
And I am happy!

The Only Job That Matters

The only job that matters,
The hardest one of all.

Coaching, guiding, loving and
caring for you.
Praying and hoping for your future.

How do I know if I am making the
right choices
How do I know you are listening to
my words, my advice.

Why do I feel like I am failing?
Why do I cry for your future?

The only job that matters,
The hardest one of all.

Coaching, guiding, loving and
caring for you.

Praying and hoping for your future.

What Can Be Done?

What can be done?
When the motivation is gone,
When the drive is lost,
When you give up,
When you have lost all hope,
What can be done?

How do you motivate someone?
How can I get you to care?
Why do I care more about your
future than you do?

What can be done?
When the motivation is gone,
When the drive is lost,
When you give up,
When you have lost all hope,
What can be done?

What can be done?

When you have lost all hope?

It is Okay to Cry!

Don't cry!
Things might be overwhelming, but you can handle them.
Don't cry!
Things might be loud, but you can handle it.
Don't cry!
Things might seem out of control, but it will be okay.

It is okay to cry!
It does not mean you are weak.
It is okay to cry!
Things can be overwhelming, but you can handle them.
It is okay to cry!

My Soul Sings

My soul sings for you.
Each day the love grows.
More than I know it could ever grow.

How could one person love someone
as much as I love you?
You have more patience and grace
than I.
Each day I see your love and it moves
my soul.

My heart warms and I wonder how I
ever became so blessed to have you
in my life.

Wake the Dragon

We are the ones you blame.
No matter what the reason.
It comes down on us.

Do you think we will always be here?
That you can blame us, and nothing will happen!
Is it because we are quiet?
Does that mean you can push us around?

I may not be outspoken,
but when I faintly speak, I get bombarded.
Was I wrong to speak my mind?
Or do you think I should stay quiet and let you continue to blame me?

You woke the sleeping dragon,
Now get ready for the fire.

Honesty and Fear

They ask you to be honest,
but is that what they really want?
When you speak honestly,
does it always work out?
Should you be honest?
Should you speak the truth?

You fear when you speak,
your heart races, will you hurt someone?
Time and time again people ask you,
to be yourself.
Do they know what they are asking for?

I am far too honest
at the wrong times.
I am insecure and,
I never think highly of myself.
I need constant reassurances and,
Often feel guilty for the things I say and do.
You say be yourself and be honest.

But the fear is overwhelming.

I am Frustrated with Myself

I am frustrated with myself.
No matter how many times someone builds me up,
My anxiety and self-doubt creep in.

Most of the time I tell myself that I am not good enough.
That I can't do this or that,
That everyone else is better than I am.

It can't be helped, after all these years.
That I would be more confident
But I'm not. I am afraid.

I am afraid of the people who love me.
That they will grow tired of my doubts.
They will grow tired of giving me affirmations,
that I don't believe
And I will lose them.

I don't want to lose them.
I love them.
I wish I was different.

The World is a Dark and Gloomy Place for Them.

The world is a dark and gloomy place for them.
Everything they touch shatters.
They long to be different.
They long to be accepted but yet they tarnish everything.
They complain about everything and everyone.
Nothing is good enough for them.
Nothing makes them happy.

I sit back and wonder.
Why do they hate so much?
We're left with unanswered questions, and insults hurled at us.

They strike out, with venom in their words.
Time and time again.
They strike out before someone strikes them.

Never accepting and never knowing what love can be.

Secrets

They fester and sore until they burst.
They warp your mind and crush your heart.
They say they are your friend and twist your words.

All the while waiting to strike.
They are quiet, and plant seeds in others.
They lay in wait in their filth.

The arrows pierce, and before you know it you are down.
The pain radiates through your being.
These secrets they keep

Why Do People Give Up on Me?

Why do people give up on me?
Am I a bad person?
That they should shun me?

I pray for my friends.
I help them when I can.
I never give up on a friend. It's not in my nature.

If I haven't heard from you in a long time,
I reached out to you.
I reached out to you.
I never give up on a friend.
It's not in my nature.

When you are alone, you will remember me.
You will remember that I never gave up on you.

But you gave up on me.
For I am only here when no one else is.

But still, I am here.
I never give up on a friend.
It's not in my nature.

When is Enough, Enough?

How long do you reach out to someone?
How long do you call someone a friend?
Do you continue to pray even when they don't care about you?

When they tarnish your name,
When they won't talk to you,
When they ignore you,
How long do you wait?

Do you still pray?
Is it wrong to move on and not care?

Isn't it hard not to care?
Are you a horrible person if you move on?

Why do I feel guilty?
Shouldn't you pray for your enemies and friends alike?
Shouldn't you be the better person?
When is it enough?
When will it ever be enough?

My Baby

Today would have been your birthday. You were due on May 20th, 2009. The loss never truly goes away.
I think of you a lot, but I know you are in good hands. Until we meet again, my angel.

Sometimes

Sometimes I need to step away.
Retreat in the darkness and hide.
Sometimes I need the quiet.
A place where no light can hit me.
Sometimes, I just need to step away.

But other times, I love the light.
I want to be loud and bright
To go to a place that is loud and full of life.
To laugh, dance and sing.

But sometimes the quiet is all I need.

Only A Number

Remember you are just a number.
No matter how much you give, you are just a number
No matter how much time you give, you are just a number.

Remember it is not about others.
It is about the impact you make.
It is about the lives you change

You might just be a number to them,
But you are a life changer to others.

Meaningless

The time I put in was meaningless.
Talking to them, listening to them, letting them cry to me.
Listening to them cry, complain as any friend would do.

Do you change who you are?
Not be a good friend to others?
No, of course not.

Those who chose to replace a friend like me,
Lose in the end.
Those who chose to replace a friend like me,

Lose the person who will do anything for them.
Lose the one who would stand up for you.
Lose the person who checks on you.
Lost the person who cares about you.

Their loss and another person's gain.

Things Done for Good

Sometimes nothing you do works.
Sometimes you try your best.
Sometimes it's better not to say anything.
Sometimes you feel like crap.

Things done for good, are always good.
Things done to help others are still good.
Things are not always what they seem
A good deed can still be a good deed.
Hold your head up high.

You help someone, but it's not enough.
You help someone, but they say you don't care.
You help someone, but they say you don't give enough.

Do you stop helping?
Close yourself off?
Change who you are?
Or keep going?

All a Lie

They say work hard.
They say good things come to those who wait.
They say do good in school.
They say work hard.

They don't know what they are talking about.
They have money, and power.
They have connections and resources.

They tell us to work hard.
But we know that it won't work
It is all a big lie.

They Say

They say work hard.
They say good things come to those who wait.
They say do good in school.
They say work hard.

They don't know what they are talking about.
They have money, and power.
They have connections and resources.

They tell us to work hard.
But we know that it won't work
It is all a big lie.

I am Strong

I am strong.
I will prevail.
I am powerful.
My words can move mountains.
My words can tear people down.
I chose to lift them up.

I am strong.
I am loved.
I am beautiful.
My words can move mountains.
My words can tear people down.
I chose to lift them up.

What Depression Feels Like

What Depression Feels Like
The water is so warm around me.
Fills me with such warmth and love.
Slowly I feel it move,
Down and down it goes.
The cold hitting my body
As the warmth recedes
Soon I am laying in a cold bath,
Wondering where the warmth has gone.

I See the Phone

I see the phone,
I could pick it up and call.
I could message more, but
I am paralyzed.

I twirl my hair till there is a
mark on my fingers
and my hair curls from all
the twirling.
My heart races, and I can't
breathe,
Still life carries on.

I do not call,
I hate the phone,

I try to message,
But I think I am a bother.

This is anxiety.

Give Up

My heart is open,
The doors are too.
But only one is knocking,
Only one is calling.

Is this the point when you give up?
Is this the point when you need to stop?

The leaves turn from green to brown
And then fall away and die.
They can no longer fight change than i.

Is this the time to let go?
Allow others to leave your life?
Pray they coming knocking?
Leave it up to them?

Will they know that I care?
To is it too late for that?

My heart is open,
The doors are too.
But only one is knocking,
Only one is calling.

My Surprise

My husband surprised me one night when I was feeling really stressed and not good enough. He wrote me a poem, and anyone who knows me knows that I love poetry. I in turn wrote one for him.

I want you to know (From My husband to me)

I want you to know
I will always be here
Through good times
And the bad ones too
I will stand with you
I will love you
Until the end of my days
I want you to know
There is nothing in this world
That can change how I feel
How special you are

How lucky i feel to have you in my life
I want you to know.
Just how amazing you are
How much love you have in your heart
How talented you are
I want you to know I love you babe

His Surprise

My husband surprised me one night when I was, and this is the poem I wrote for him. (This is not the first one I wrote for him, but it made me feel so loved that he wrote one for me.

I want you to know
How creative you are.
How forgiving you are
How patient you are

I look at you and I see
All the goodness that God has placed in you
Nothing in this life will ever take me from you.

I will be with you in the good
times and the bad

I want you to know
How understanding
how compassionate,
and how loyal you are

I want you to know
How lucky I am to have found
you
How blessed I am that you are in
my life.

A Flower

A flower blooms
Spreading its petals out to enjoy the sun.
The sun rises and sets
Each day a new day

Each day a new chance for change,
Each day a new chance for greatness
Each day a new chance to fund your passion.

The flower blooms taking in the sun.
Spreading its joys for all to see.
Be the flower and spread your petals, for all to see.

Always

Always asking if I did it right
Always worried about how others see me.
Always correcting to make everyone happy.

Do you like what I did there?
Do I need to change it?
Do you like how I wrote that?

The rejection,
The anticipation,
The need to be the best.

When will I be enough?
When will I be good enough?
When will criticism not get to me?

About the Author

Nancy Ann is a writer, teacher, poet, & mother. She enjoys reading interesting stories and writing poetry, paranormal fiction, & sci-fi.

Nancy attended Asbury University for her undergraduate and Stockton University for graduate school, where she majored in special education and history and English.

Originally from NJ, she currently teaches in Kentucky and lives, and writes, in Indiana with her family.

Nancy has always had stories in her head but felt writing an entire book was too overwhelming and feared she would not be good at it or be able to finish writing one. It wasn't until she experienced a tremendous loss of a miscarriage that she began to write. Wiring helped her overcome one of the darkest moments of her life. Nancy wanted to help other women who were going through this awful experience.

Now with newly added coincidence, Nancy started writing paranormal fiction, poetry as well as science fiction. She had many books out now and more to write. Stay tuned for more and never give up on your dream.

Made in United States
Orlando, FL
14 May 2023